"Just Ask"

by
Sue Chandler

Cover Illustration by
Kelly Barrow

AuthorHouse™

1663 Liberty Drive
Bloomington, IN 47403
www.authorhouse.com
Phone: 1-800-839-8640

© *2010 Sue Chandler. All rights reserved.*

No part of this book may be reproduced, stored in a retrieval system, or transmitted by any means without the written permission of the author.

First published by AuthorHouse   3/22/2010

ISBN: 978-1-4490-7399-2 (e)
ISBN: 978-1-4490-7398-5 (sc)

Library of Congress Control Number: 2010900451

Printed in the United States of America
Bloomington, Indiana

This book is printed on acid-free paper.

"Over There" Productions
(Owner Sue Chandler)

Presents
"JUST ASK"
Author
SUE CHANDLER

Edited by
Elaine Magee
BrittMarie

Preface by
His Holiness Grandmaster Lin Yun

"JUST ASK"

CONSIOUS SYMBOLS, A WAY TO CONNECT WITH SOURCE

CONTENTS

PREFACE   xv

INTRODUCTION   xvii

PART I   LEARNING ABOUT SELF

- What are we? Energy, Vibrations, Inter dimensional Beings.   1

PART II   YOUR INTERNAL ENERGY SYSTEM

- The Chakras and Our Auras   3
- Harmony, Alignment and Balance   5
- Grounding   6
- How to ground Working with your energy   6

PART III   SYMBOLOGY, THE UNIVERSAL LANGUAGE OF COMMUNICATION.

- Finding your strongest way of communicating with source energy or your God.   9
- Being in the Dark   11
- For the Left Brained Logical Human   12
- Meditation, Breath and Prayer   12
- Appreciation   13

PART IV   THE PROCESS

- A conscious Connection (Apposed to a dream state)   15
- Step by step process on how to get the symbols and signs.   15

PART V SYMBOLS DICTIONARY

Chapter 1	Animals, Birds, Fish, Incects, Reptiles & Rodents, Animals	21
Chapter 2	Clothing	36
Chapter 3	Equipment, Tools & Things with Wheels	40
Chapter 4	Food and Beverages	45
Chapter 5	Games (ALL TYPES)	52
Chapter 6	Items Found In Home	57
Chapter 7	Nature	67
Chapter 8	People and Occupations	70
Chapter 9	Signs	78
Chapter 10	Sports (All Types)	82
Chapter 11	Miscellaneous	103

PART VI CHANGE — **113**

PART VII YOU CAN DO IT, YOU CAN DO IT, YOU CAN, YOU CAN. YOU CAN, YOU CAN! — **115**

AUTHOR BIO

Sue Chandler led a traditional life opening and directing three day care centers and being an elementary school secretary. Being a visionary she started many programs in her community for the children. Her joy/purpose has always been about her two sons and all the children.

Having Multiple Sclerosis, (MS) Sue left the school district in 1995 and experienced her natural gifts and talents come flooding in. She became an active "Medium" as well as brought the enlightened Crystal Children onto the planet. Becoming a Reiki Master teacher and running a volunteer Reiki healing clinic, helped in the healing of her MS.

Not stopping there, she assisted in starting up a massage school, became a certified massage therapist and a Universal Life Force Minister, all of which was connected to her active Medium-ship.

Sue's life experiences and being "Grandma Sue" to her three grandchildren healed her after having quintuple bypass heart surgery.

She has much appreciation for being here on this beautiful planet. Internationally as well as state wide, Sue has touched many lives with her readings, healings and teachings. It has always been her intent to empower others in finding their own greatness and spiritual gifts.

Now being an Author, this book is her gift to the universe. Sue asks that you have fun with the process. Love, Laugh and find JOY in all things. Who knows what life holds for you after reading this book.

Remember ... YOU ARE MAGNIFICENT!!!

DEDICATION

"JUST ASK"

I dedicate to all of
Y O U !!!!!

ACKNOWLEDGEMENT

My great appreciation to my God, the magnificent spirits, guides, angels and masters on this and other dimensions, who assisted me in presenting this joyous "simplified" process accelerating all aspects of our ascension.

To the following who freely gave of their gifts, love and support allowing this book to come into fruition.

His Holiness Professor Lin Yun, her Holiness Crystal Chu Rinopche, and staff, George, my sons Tim, Mike Daughter-in laws Kim and Sarah, my dear grandchildren Dylan, Braelyn and Darin., Kathy, Elaine and girls, Stacey, Jennifer, Bill, Brittany, Madeline, Joseph, Nancy, Ron, Sheryl, Tom, Jim, Brian, BrittMarie, Sanjay, Vivian, Jane, Mimi, Cheryl, Cathy, Carrie, June, Dr. John, Dr. Kananaugh, Dr. Kamlot. Dr. DeMonterio, Melissa, Joan, Rich, Eileen, David, Robert, Charlie, Nick, Michelle, Madonna, Cindy, Kim, Laura, Sandy, Dee, Deb, Digger, The Martinez family, Lurdis, Diamond, Judy, Avelino, Rob, Angelica, Paola, Kevin and Lindsay, Gary, Linda, Lilly, Geoff, Mary, Jennie, Crystal, Betty, Ken, Rey. Share, Gail, Author House Staff, and the many friends not mentioned.

You know who you are. Thank You! Dreams do come true with a little help from my friends.

I appreciate you!   Sue

PREFACE

by His Holiness Grandmaster Lin Yun

JUST FROM LOOKING at the name of this book, you would know that its content is all-inclusive and covers everything. It is as the author, Sue Chandler is saying magnanimously, "Go ahead, just ask away!" In life you are bound to encounter many difficulties, and be it career, relationship, marriage, academic studies, interpersonal relationships, lawsuits, promotion, or loss of wealth, you will find a suitable answer. It is up to you to follow the path of this right answer, and you will rise again and see the light of day. When one has exhausted all resources and comes to a dead end, there will be a new hope, which offers a new direction.

This book allows us to first understand ourselves, and then to use that understanding to discover our latent abilities and channel our own energies. Each of us has, within our own bodies, our own spiritual light, or the so-called "chakra." Chakra is a straight line in your body that encompasses love, harmony, and balance, and this line can communicate with the heavens above. It is a message from the simultaneous resonance with the universe. The author studies how, by sitting in the dark and using meditation, breathing, prayers, and a thankful heart, we can find the strongest method of communicating with the source of energy. Furthermore, it allows those of us who are used to using the logic of the left brain to make cognitive connection to symbols and signs. In the first eleven chapters of the dictionary of symbols, we are introduced to animals, insects, birds, fish, human clothing, and tools, apparatus and equipment, items with wheels, dining, games, and a variety of interesting household items. Then, according to your own profession and personality, there are various signs as regulated by society, law, and morals. There are also rules and regulations about sports, as well as many others, which show us how to part with tradition. In all, you must strengthen your "self confidence" and trust yourself. When there is a will, there is a way. You should have faith that you have the power to directly control and discipline your thoughts and your spiritual power.

Therefore I believe that just by opening this book, you will receive benefits. This is a sacred work that will bring salvation to many people, old and young. The ancients say, "Do one good deed per day." The publication of this book has the effect of doing ten or a hundred good deeds per day. Her Holiness Crystal Chu Rinpoche, the supreme leader of the Black Sect Tantric Buddhism Fifth Stage, knows that urgent matters demand that I fly to Taipei immediately, but she has been keeping a watchful eye on me to finish this foreword as soon as possible. I have since sacrificed many hours of sleep and happy moments in order to finish this assignment, and feel quite joyous and comforted to know that I have given my thoughts on Sue's new book.

Lin Yun

Retiring Supreme Leader of the Black Sect Tantric Buddhism Fourth Stage

At *Zi Hong Hsuan*, the study of the Lady Zi Hong (the pen name of Khadro Crystal Chu Rinpoche)

His Holiness Grandmaster Lin Yun has been credited with introducing and bringing Feng Shui from China to the United States, as well as performing Feng Shui on the White House.

INTRODUCTION

WHAT YOU ARE about to read is A WAY to connect to Source, God, Mother Father God, your Higher Self, or who ever you wish to call a Higher Power. I hold no attachments to being right or wrong, it just is. Scientists have said that approximately 15% of the human brain is being actively used leaving 85% untapped. Becoming conscious or awakened to our thoughts and tuning in with our feelings and emotions helps us tap into the unused 85%. By doing this we are propelled to a level of consciousness where we will begin to see the universal symbols in our every day life. Everywhere you are, for example, there are symbols to help you understand and to remember what a magnificent being you are. If the symbols appear less then you would like them to be, you get the chance to change it and evolve into a more loving, well balanced, enlightened, healthy, and happy spirit.

In presenting this process, it is my intent to have fun getting in touch with Source energy, God, or ones Higher Self. Nobody knows you better than you. Find the best feeling in the process and go with it.

If you are reading this book then you are ready to take your next step.

PART I
LEARNING ABOUT SELF

What and who are we really?

Everything is a vibration, or Energy. Those vibrations are compiled and make up matter, even humans. The grids are like the basic energy blueprints or map of the universe. We as humans are both physical and non-physical beings. We have made an agreement to come to earth and create, to evolve as spirits and assist in the earth's evolution. We are very powerful beings and we have all been created from the same source energy.

We have been here on earth many times before with family members and friends. We also have shared some of these lives as what we judge to be Good and Bad people. You have been it all my friends. Energy is energy. It just is. So when you point the finger in judgment at someone else, look at your hand, there are three more fingers pointing back at you. How exciting for this lifetime you get to deal with your own lessons, your own stuff and your own wonderful creations. Let others enjoy their life as it has been created for them. You could say that we have been thinking GREEN long before now. Over and over again we have been recycling our lives. There once was a time when I was not sure if I believed in reincarnation and the gifts of Clairaudience, etc. There is no doubt for me now, being a Medium/intuitive that I have been guided and shown how to tap into all energies on the universal grids. That answered my question when a client would ask me to connect with someone who had passed to the other side or is still on the planet for that matter, "How could I connect and speak with that spirit, that vibration of someone I never knew in any way, shape or form before?" We are all special and unique beings. There is nobody like you nor will there ever be anyone like you. Nobody is better then anyone else. We reincarnate and get to create different experiences so we can evolve and return to play once again.

PART II
YOUR INTERNAL ENERGY SYSTEM

THE CHAKRAS

By knowing about ones Chakras, learning to keep them in balance, in alignment, and keeping them clear, we are able to interpret the symbols with clarity and be able to find love and joy in our lives.

In this book I will be referring to only the basic seven Chakras, their opening, and the flow of life force energy through them. Each one plays a pivotal part in our being. The colors change all the time, the colors are what some see as energy flowing throughout our bodies systems .We also have and use Chakra in our hands, knees, and feet. These combined are known as ones Aura or energy field.

CHAKRAS

1. Located at the tailbone area.
   Associated with survival issues.
   Color Red.

2. Located in the abdomen area.
   Associated with relationships.
   Color Orange.

3. Located in the stomach area and is known also known as The Solar Plexus.
   Associated with personal power.
   Color Yellow.

Chakras one through three are known as the bottom chakras. Here is a way to keep them balanced and starting the alignment process. Each one should be opened to a size that feels good for you.

A good size for the first and second charkas to be opened to is about the size of a baby food jar lid. The third chakra usually feels good when opened to the size of a mayonnaise jar lid. Sometimes when this chakra is wide open, one can feel vulnerable and powerless. (How to adjust them will be shown below).

4. The heart chakra located in between the breasts.
   Associated with Love.
   Colors Green and Pink.

5. Located in the throat area.
   Associated with Communication.
   Color Baby Blue.

6. Located in the middle of the eyebrows
   Associated with Clairvoyance, intuition Imagination, (also known as your (Third eye).
   Color Indigo Blue.

7. The Crown
   Located in the middle top of head
   Associated with Knowledge, wisdom and understanding.
   Color Violet (purple).

Chakra's four through seven are known as the upper Charkas. Their size is up to the individuals feelings. If your heart is hurting for example, close it by visualizing them spinning clockwise (closing it). The opposite, counter clockwise for opening the chakras.

The Aura is comprised of all of the Chakra. It tells all about you. To the trained eye, It shakes when you are not speaking the truth. Look up at the moon, you will see clearly what an Aura looks like. Do you see that light around the outline of the moon? This is the moon's Aura. Everyone and everything has an Aura. Some pictures of Jesus, will show you his Aura. They look like halos over his head.

I was shown Auras one day while walking in a department store, all of a sudden, everything and everyone had a glow around them, Wow, how beautiful. I am shown them now only when I ask to see them or when it will serve me to assist another spirit.

HARMONY, ALIGNMENT AND BALANCE

Life is all about Love. That is why we are here. Since we are made up of vibrations, energy, and it is that energy that runs through our Chakras, our internal systems, it is important to keep them running clear. Thinking happy, healthy thoughts, seeing only that which you want, allowing your energy system to flow in harmony, brings everything into alignment and balance. Working on creating joy and love in your life, allowing it to come in, manifests everything you have ever dreamed of being, doing, or having.

Working with Energy light workers such as Massage Therapists, Reiki Masters, Acupuncture, and Chiropractors just to name a few, will help with the interior flow of energy while Feng Shui will be able to work with the exterior of the self and your surroundings, allowing the energy to flow for our best and highest good. I remember hearing as a child "choose your friends wisely," surround your self with positive happy people. Being an energy worker, I now understand how we are all like sea sponges picking up all sorts of energies. We pick up others thoughts, positive and negative energy. So being in an environment of joy, now makes more sense. The phrase "you are what you eat", also rings true because food is also a vibration and some foods are light and some like Meat for instance, is a heavier vibration. So be conscious of whom you are around and what you eat and "Just Ask" how am I feeling? Remember there must be a balance of all things for us to be in alignment. When interior and exterior energies are in balance, you will be in perfect alignment. Working with the flow of energy, remembering that everything is energy, a vibration, we can remain clear, clutter free, light, balanced, aligned and connected with Source or God.

GROUNDING

Grounding is a very important tool for us humans to use. Have you ever seen a hot wire flailing about and make a hissing noise? That is exactly like us. Being electricity, if we are not grounded and connected, we are going in 15 different directions, scattering our energy everywhere. Do you know someone who has difficulty finishing anything, remaining focused long enough to complete the task at hand? I have my hand raised up very high right now. I would start all sorts of projects and never complete most of them. I used to say that it was just creativity. While that's true, without the action of the thought and the completion, nothing ever gets finished. You can also add a procrastinator in the mix as well. However this has changed. Grounding puts you in the present moment and allows your energy to flow. If you are not grounded, people can knock you off balance. If they were to push your shoulder and you were not grounded, your body would move to the side, you'd know you have been moved. Being grounded and someone comes up to you and pushes you, you will be solid and not move. That has allowed you to be in the "NOW" or in the present, focused on what you are so wanting to accomplish. You are in control, not someone else.

HOW TO GROUND
WORKING WITH YOUR ENERGY

First place your feet firmly on the ground. Visualize in your mind's eye, a tree trunk or anchor and screwing one end tightly to your tail bone. Now drop it straight down into the core of the earth (not backwards that is the past or ahead being the future). Open your feet Chakra, counter clockwise. Now on the IN breath, bring up the earths energy up your legs to the first Chakra, at the same time visualize the golden suns energy going down from your opened 7th Chakra down the back of your spine, clearing Chakras and blending with the 1st Chakra's energy. On the OUT breath send some down your grounding cord to the core of the earth, knowing it will transmute into pure light and also on the OUT breath take the remaining energy, sending it up the front of your Chakras spilling out the 7th Chakra, clearing your aura.

PART III
SYMBOLOGY, THE UNIVERSAL LANGUAGE OF COMMUNICATION.

Not everyone speaks the language of this book, however everyone can recognize and interpret symbols that are universal and appear in our everyday lives. Everywhere you look there are symbols to help you understand your life.

FINDING YOUR STRONGEST WAY OF COMMUNICATING WITH SOURCE ENERGY OR YOUR GOD.

We are all intuitive and psychic. We are all clairvoyants. Clairvoyant is a catch - all word for our gifts, "that are of sight, hearing and feeling on a daily basis". It excites me to learn that we can interpret life's messages any time and anywhere. We just have to ask. You do not have to have a Masters Degree to read the Universal Symbols and Signs. Actually we are all Masters here on this beautiful Earth.

There are different ways however that each one effortlessly seems to receive the symbols given us. (Note, these are the most commonly used).

    Clairvoyant-   Seeing

    Clairaudient -   Hearing

    Clairsentience - Feeling

However we can use them all. The following is an example of using all of the different ways in a short time.

EXAMPLE

I was giving a reading to one of my clients when the "Number 16" came from a distance and was moving towards me. (Seeing). I asked what did the "Number 16" mean to her? She indicated that her daughter was 16 years old. That must have been the correct interpretation because I immediately heard the word "SPAM", (Hearing) and asked what did the word "SPAM" meant to her? She said that her daughter had been in a SPAM commercial when she was younger. I got a very worried feeling come over me (Feeling), so I said, your daughter is worried about you, give her a call when we are done here. She did and indeed her daughter asked where she was that she was worried about her not being home. So you see how the symbols arrive and how they can be interpreted in different ways.

Some of us have chosen to embrace our gifts and follow our guidance. (Example) I discovered my channeling ability one day while lying on the couch hearing a voice telling me to get up after viewing these pictures (like a movie) and document that which was being shown me. It was a geometric configuration with a template code. I thought to myself, why am I being given this information, I barely passed Algebra. I asked, "Who is giving me this information"? I heard IMRA. I was explaining to my roommate at the time, all about that which I had just channeled including that which I had been asked to write down. It was no surprise to her and she started to explain that I had been channeling RA, the sun God of Egypt. The next day my friend brought over a book for me to read. It was about the RA Channeling. In the book explained that

RA responded to questions asked of him with the response, "I AM RA" Well there was my IMRA I heard earlier. This is what I mean by being conscious and open. I could have overlooked this important message and missed a life changing event for me.

It makes no difference if you are religious, educated, what part of the world you come from or what age you are, we can all receive and interpret symbols on some level. The miracles come when we are really grounded, conscious and aware of the guidance being giving us.

A great example of this is a newborn baby. Babies interpret your energy right off the bat.

Babies react appropriately. They are eager to only feel good, so they break the pattern (Pattern interrupt) by crying loudly, changing the mood and getting your attention consciously. You feel their sadness and discomfort, proceed to pick them up and might say "Oh now now, its going to be all right". They know what they are doing. The babies and young children are on the planet at this time are here to teach and heal us and in doing so help with the evolution of earth and those on it.

BEING IN THE DARK

The story of Helen Keller being blind, and deaf is a beautiful story of surrendering that which we consider a normal way of communicating with each other. Through sight, hearing and speaking, most of us get our words across to one and other. We are much like Helen Keller in the fact that many of us do not see, hear or speak our truth. There is a whole new world to tap into out there. With a little change in our consciousness, we can change how we view life as we know it. Until you can connect the words with the symbols and signs to their meaning in the physical, you to are in the dark. With "JUST ASK", you will have a brand new picture, auditory, feeling dictionary at your disposal 24 hours a day, 7 days a week to assist you in your daily life.

FOR THE LEFT BRAINED LOGICAL HUMAN

The "Brain" is the thought, inside the skull. (Matter) Your "Mind" is your spiritual part of you outside of the physical brain. Growing up I heard the phrase, "Mind over Matter" and often wondered what that meant. I really had no idea the meaning of the phrase until later in life. How the process works scientifically is as follows.

On the IN breath the Brain opens and indulges in thinking. On a certain wave length or channel, then on the OUT breath, the mind brings in the symbol which we can then interpret.

It is much like wanting to hear the football game on the radio station KNBR Channel 680 on your AM dial, or wanting to listen to the country western station the Wolf on 95.7 F.M. Both are great to listen to, however to channel the station of your choice, you would have to be on the same wave length or vibration to connect.

MEDITATION, BREATH AND PRAYER

These three go together for me. When you sit quietly take a few deep breaths, you are connecting to source or your God. It is then when we can clear our brain of what is referred to sometimes as the "Monkey Mind" of all the chatter and nonsense not needed, or serving you.

Often we find ourselves going to bed and rehashing over and over again the day we had just encountered. For that matter, many keep telling the same old stories about the past, over and over again as well. What this does is reactivate their thought process and you relive it over and over again. Enough already. To change this process, consciously change the thought and deactivate it by taking in a few deep breaths and think of something enjoyable, calming down, embellish on the thought for a little longer then a minute. By tapping in and connecting to this energy, it will allow you to change and be able to move forward and eliminating that which is no longer serving you.

I always like to "Just Ask" what is my next step? What should I focus on today? Then I am able to set my intentions for the day. We have the power to directly control and discipline our thoughts and spiritual power as referred to by his Holiness Grand Master Lin Yun, who wrote the preface for this book.

Having music in the background, (Tone) also detracts and does a pattern interrupt or (P.I.) along with deep breathing, clears out some clutter.

Making time each day to connect. to Source, by taking a walk, finding time to sit quietly and breath, say mantras, recite some verses out of their Bibles, listen to music or hum, are all forms of meditation. Praying is a way to show our appreciation for those around us and the abundance of gifts we have been given. We are able to have positive thoughts for those who are seeking additional love and healing in their lives.

APPRECIATION

We are very much loved and blessed. It is so important to be grateful for all that has been given us in the past and those people who have assisted our soul growth and continue to do so. We really only have this moment in time to count our blessings, yet it would not hurt to pay ahead and appreciate that which is coming into fruition in the future.

To help manifest your hearts desire, you could say your positive affirmations daily, followed by your gratitude affirmations as well. Sitting in a long line of traffic each morning I would say at least 30 affirmations. On my return trip I would say my gratitude's for all I had been given during that day. Usually when my head hits the pillow I am gone for the count, so I feel it is all apart of my gratitude for being here on the planet. When I am walking in the mornings it feels good to bless all the people I know, as well as those I don't, all of nature, along with all the cars passing me by. Wishing them a joyous, healthy, prosperous day. This is also a great time to do the grounding exercises and the PROCESS Part 1V of this book.

I also enjoy letting people know that I appreciate them for something. They have just done or said.

EXAMPLE   I speak my truth.

It feels good. I am honored to be able to write this book for the Universe. To the many who have added their loving energy and made this book come into fruition, my deepest heartfelt THANKS to you all.

PART IV
THE PROCESS

THIS PROCESS CAN be done by yourself or with others asking the same question, allowing different aspects of the question resulting in more information to be delivered. Get GROUNDED. Be quiet and still. By getting grounded, you will be allowing yourself to receive the symbol with the up most clarity. You will be in the present moment. (IN THE NOW). It is in this state that Miracles happen.

IT IS MOST IMPORTANT TO KEEP YOUR EYES OPEN.

DURING THIS PROCESS. THIS IS A <u>CONSCIOUS</u> WAY OF ATTAINING THE ANSWERS THROUGH SYMBOLS.

STEP ONE

<u>Slowly</u> take a deep breath through the nose

filling the stomach, abdomen and lungs. Hold it for a few

seconds then <u>slowly</u> release the breath though the mouth. Repeat this three times. (This will allow the brain to open and clear the channels for the Mind to accept the response).

STEP TWO

Get ready to ask your question. Think about how you are going to word the question. Remember it is to be only one question at a time.

This is where most people jump ahead of the process. It would be great if you used mostly open ended questions, allowing more detailed information to come in to you through symbols. (YES, NO, and time related questions may also be asked.)

EXAMPLE

"Am I going to get a raise?" (Yes – No) Example: "What month am I going to get my raise?" Now you might be shown a calendar with the month on it, or you may get a number indicating the Number 3, then ask again, "Is it 3 months from now?" The next question, "Am I getting my raise in March?" Another question might be ,"What year am I going to get this raise?" You can keep digging deeper and ask "How much your raise will be?" Etc.

STEP THREE

Now gather others that may be assisting you and start: All of you on the IN Breath ask the decided question to ask and speak out loud the question in Unison. Get ready for on the OUT breath the very first thing that you are conscious of, is your answer. The out breath may be released slowly or with a quick abrupt release. You may feel something, shown something, hear something, or as some of you may feel that you just had imagined it.

THAT IS YOUR ANSWER, THE VERY FIRST THING THAT COMES TO YOU. THAT IS YOUR GUIDANCE. THAT IS THE

CONNECTING TO SOURCE. T R U S T IN THE "JUST ASK" PROCESS. YOU GOT IT. GREAT JOB!

STEP FOUR

Now here is the fun part. Go around the room and find out what everyone got. Write the SYMBOLS down. Now look up the symbols in the symbols section of this book and retrieve their meaning. Put them all together and get your answers to your most important question.

REMEMBER MOST OF US GET SYMBOLS OR SIGNS ACCORDING TO OUR PROFESSIONS, HOBBIES AND OUR OWN PERSONALITIES.

EXAMPLE

Three people gathered to get an answer for a women. Her question was as follows. "What is the transition going to be like returning to work after just having had surgery?"

So the three of us did the PROCESS and the response was as follows. I got the symbol "Cheerleaders," Being a Motivational Speaker.

The second person got the symbol "1/2", he is general contractor and uses fractions on his job.

The women asking the question got the symbol "A Lake" she often would go sailing on her favorite lake.

The answer to her question.

She will be returning back to work as her colleagues are cheering her on welcoming her back to work. She will be going back to work part time for a while, ½ days maybe, and in asking her what the lake looked like, her response was it was smooth as glass, which means she will have a smooth transition going back to work.

NOW HOW MUCH MORE FUN CAN THIS PROCESS BE?

PART V
SYMBOLS DICTIONARY

The dictionary of symbols is Channeled information showing A Way to interpret symbols, remember however, there is no one more qualified to interpret your feelings than YOU!!! Trust and believe in yourself.

I was shown that sometimes you can dissect the words given. You will find a (D) in front of these definitions.

SYMBOLS DICTIONARY

CHAPTER 1
ANIMALS, BIRDS, FISH, INCECTS, REPTILES & RODENTS, ANIMALS

ANTELOPE	Fast moving, (D) Can elope, small amount attending wedding.
ANTEATER	(D) Eat smaller bites to digest what is happening.
ARMADILLO	A need to shield oneself, blinded putting arm up not to see something coming or right in front of you.
BEARS	Strength, hibernation, a need to sleep on it before making a decision, go within self and meditate.
BADGER	Some one is forcing their will on you or others, being bullied.
BUFFALO	Symbol of old strength, your are being taken advantage of.
BLACK PANTHER	Quick movement in the darkness, female figure, sleek, high vibration.
CATS (Types)	Great healers, independent, a need to listen more and purr, then speak up now, to find balance one must relax and purr and be joyous right where they are at that moment.

	BLACK	Divine Feminine/ intriguing / mysterious.
	ALLEY	Thinking dark and narrow thoughts.
	MANX	Condense something, keep it short.
	CALICO	Multi-faceted, Need to patch things up.
	KITTEN	Young, inexperienced, playful.

COW
(Types)

	DAIRY	Speak up and be heard, helps keep planet strong and healthy,(D) how dare he.
	LONG HORNED	A person from Texas, related to big things, stuck, bullish, controlling, ready to stand ones ground and fight for what one is intending.
	COYOTE	Someone is pretending to be one thing, but really represents something or some one else.
	DEER	Gentleness, blinded, not being able to see entire picture.

DOGS
(Types)   Loyalty, protection issue, a need to exercise.

	BOXER	Fighting, clinched fists, anger. (D) keeping her silent.

BULL DOG	Bully Type of personality. Grumpy, someone short in stature, buffed, solid, firm, strong.
GOLDEN RETRIEVERS	Represents unconditional love, the need to fetch something.
LAB	Playful, fun loving, still in experimental stage.
POODLE	High strung, fru fru nose in the air Type individual. Feels as if he/she is better then others.
ELEPHANT	Strong willed, time to take deliberate steps to goal, can take care of own needs, power.
FOX	A sly maneuver, a situation moving along quickly, look at its integrity, looks nice from the outside appearance, there is more information or substance not revealed.
GIRAFFE	A visionary, take a look at the bigger picture, rise above the situation or person.
GOAT	Someone is butting heads.
HORSE	Loyal, detector of danger of some kind, time to move on.
JAGUAR	High maintenance and sleek individual, quick to change mind.
KANGAROO	Messenger, only moves forward, defends self by kicking and screaming, tantrum.

LAMB	Be more gentle with self or others.
LION	Someone of importance is speaking, listen up, it may be a protection issue.
LYNX	(D) Look where the links are in situation and take note where one is missing or weak.
MOOSE	Big headed, strength, hang in there.
MOUNTAIN LION	(D) Top person, CEO, owner, in control of project or situation.
OPOSSUM	Someone hanging around playing dead as if not paying attention, wrong, however is a carrier of lots of information, something is hung up.
PORCUPINE	Respect issue, someone may be needling you to see the point of something.
RABBIT	Situation will be duplicating itself quickly, get a move on, soft and cuddly.
RACCOON	There is a masking of information or a person trying to steal information, there is a cover up, something has dissolved.
SHEEP	Follower, person is not thinking for themselves, maybe not such a warm fuzzy feeling after all.
SKUNK	Respect, a warning is given to look and listen if not a stinky situation may develop.

TIGER	Male energy attacking someone in the way, pouncing, moving forward, heed the tone of voice it is a warning.
WOLF	Strong male energy, protector of pack or group you are in or dealing with, scouts.
ZEBRA	Ying-Yang energy, balanced, one can only see something as black or white.

BIRDS
(Types)

BLACK BIRD	Female energy, smaller version of Crow or Raven, balancing the Ying-Yang energy in the room or location in question.
BLUEBIRD	Healing energy. Something, someone needs healing, emotions involved.
BLUE JAY	Person is screeching at you, listen up, wanting to get a point across to you.
CANARY	Spreading of light, sunshine.
CARDINAL	Reminder to release or surrender survival issues, First Chakra (D) denial of receiving self, of prosperity and abundance, person in charge.
CHICKADEE	Term of endearment. Youthful, young.
CHICKEN	Loss of courage.
CRANE	High vibration, visionary, being able to see whole picture, birth of new situation.

CROW	Magical, Mystical, way shower, gives direction or information in the most direct way.
CUCKOO	One who does not follow the norm, possibly a Genius IQ, time to pay attention to task at hand.
DOVE	Symbol of peace, balance of male and female, indicates love and good will in this situation or relationship.
DUCK	(D) Bend down for you are being attacked in some way, someone continues to move forward and nothing slows him down.
EAGLE (Types)	
BALD	Highest vibration, has attained respect and honor, older wisdom, a visionary. One can see refined details. Soaring.
GOLDEN	High vibration, light worker, eager to teach, rich vocabulary, flies high.
EMU	Old thinking, grounded, a person holding a lot of weight. Wisdom.
FALCON	(D) Delivering a low vibration message, someone not speaking the truth.
FINCH	(D) caught unaware, quick movements.

FLICKER	(D) The female needs to wake up and pay attention to what is being said or action taking place around her.
GROUSE	(D) Something is unattractive to you.
HAWK	Great visionary, eye sight may need to be checked. Circles main subject or event. High Vibration, watching over you.
HERON	Intelligent, right on with answers, comes to the rescue.
HUMMINGBIRD	Someone quick, darts in and out. Messenger. Looking for sweetness.
KINGFISHER	Top person searching for answers.
MAGPIE	The gossip, always in others business or lives, likes hearing own voice, messenger of information.
MEADOWLARK	Happiness and joy being spread to large area.
MINER	Repetition, one likes hearing themselves speak, attention getter, loud, digs deep to find meaning of situation.
MOCKINGBIRD	(D) Being made fun of, someone is not happy with your actions, being made to feel less than, repetitive.
NUTHATCH	(D) Someone was very hard headed, opinionated and has finally awakened to see an others viewpoint or more of the bigger picture.

ORIOLE	It is all or nothing situation.
OSTRICH	Person who is in a high or top position has head buried, stubborn, feathers ruffled, exerting their will on others just because they can.
OWL	A wise person, very well balanced and gives a hoot about what is being asked of them.
PARROT	One who represents in a colorful way, what needs to be heard at this time.
PARAKEET	Smaller version of Parrot message above.
PEACOCK	Offering many color full choices to pick from that are right in front of you, all the cards are out to see.
PELICAN	A need to get the entire scoop to make a confident conscious choice or decision.
PENGUIN	Strutting your stuff, you can weather anything placed in front of you now.
PHEASANT	(D) Pleasant situation.
PIGEON	The messenger; be aware of signs.
QUAIL	All is in alignment, follow the leaders advise.
RAVEN	(D) You can be pleased with yourself or outcome of situation at hand. (See Crow).
ROAD RUNNER	You are on your path moving quickly.

ROBIN	New beginnings, spring into action.
ROOSTER	Male energy, strutting his stuff, ego based needing to be heard, look for the new beginnings.
SEAGULL	(D) Look at situation for you may be gullible.
SPARROW	(D) You have an extra something lined up if needed.
STORK	New beginnings, something is being delivered.
SWALLOW TAIL	(D) Having difficulty swallowing some words or something taking place, or someone is spinning you a tale.
SWAN	Grace is flowing through you and or in situation.
SWIFT	Must move quickly, there is an urgency.
SWISHER	Move the energy, look at situation from another angle.
TURKEY	(D) Be thankful, gratitude, appreciation is the true key to having a happy and joyous life. Feast or Famine.
WOODPECKER	Be attentive to the continued knocking, message being given to you, someone being hard headed.
WREN	(D) Speaking of a time (When) table.

FISH
(& Aquatic Mammals)

ANGEL FISH	Nice presence around a person, angelic in nature.
BASS	Find joy in the situation, enjoy the time you have.
BETA FISH	Someone is poking and challenging you at this time, someone looking to take over your position.
CATFISH	Feeling comfortable just lying around, having low energy.
COD	Can do in a strange manner.
CRAB	Can move easily all directions, checks things out before moving forward, multifaceted. individual.
DOLPHIN	Second Wavers, play full, leaping with joy, great communicator, time to lighten up on yourself, something, or people around you.
EEL	Slimy, a fast moving dark energy.
GOLDFISH	Abundance.
HALIBUT	Movement is required here.
HAMMERHEAD SHARK	Someone is trying to get your attention, attack, the pounding in of a point.

HARBOR SEAL	(D) Hold onto things, barking at life, the holding of grudges.
JELLY FISH	Stings, shaky or sticky situation.
KOI	Being shy, not speaking up.
MANATEE	Bridger from one thing, time or space to another, Visionary, full of playfulness, child like. Communicator between two or more of something.
MINNOW	Lots of little things bothering you, following directions, doing it only one way.
PIRANHA	Looks are deceiving. Ready to attack.
RED SNAPPER	Snap to it now, it is regards to a survival issue (first chakra).
SALMON	Going against flow of life, person who colors outside the lines. Sensual.
SEA HORSE	Racing, competition. Completion assured.
SEA OTTER	(D) Look at your next step. What are you are being guided to do?
STARFISH	(D) Bright, in the flow of life. Can grow and start all over again.
STURGEON	(D) Mixing something up, error not detected.
SWORDFISH	Defense, cut up, a need to cut things in smaller pieces. Dissect all parts.

TROUT	Fresh outlook on situation, colorful, in the main stream of life.
TUNA	(D) One needs a tune up, lighten diet.
WHALE	First wavers, strong communicators, beginning wisdom, keepers of DNA, balanced, Ying-Yang.

INSECTS

ANT	Many little decisions or changes make strong completion. Someone carrying more then their weight.
BEE	The sweetness of life. Your choice here to be stung or not. Look closely. Just Be.
BEETLE	Release your hard covering and listen to your inner guidance.
BUTTERFLY	Enjoy the journey and the different stages of your dreams. Note where you are in the development stage of the project and know that each step has its place and find joy in it, a transformation is taking place.
CENTIPEDE	Many ways to walk toward object or goal. Work as a team, take little steps.
CRICKET	Be aware of your situation, maybe some unexpected curves are thrown your way. Listen for the answers, be grateful, and sing praises.

DRAGONFLY	Older, wiser person guiding you. (D) Fly, do not be drug around.
GRASSHOPPER	(D) Major growth period in your life here. One may be feeling ungrounded. Know that there is hope here.
FLY	(D) Soar, to reach dreams.
KATYDID	Female energy present in completion stage.
LADYBUG	(D) There is a female energy that is annoying to you.
PRAYING MANTIS	(D) There is a very spiritual male among your surroundings.
SPIDER	(D) How dare someone spy on females actions.
WORM	(D) Some ones intention is to slowly crawl their way into your space or project.

REPTILES

ALLIGATOR/ CROCODILE	Female energy (D) Protection of young, snaps, not speaking their truth.
CHAMELEON	Someone not showing all the details camouflaging in some way.
FROG	Moving forward in a situation, taking a leap of faith, a transformation occurring.
LIZARD	Will is not strong, a person who falls in between the cracks of life.

SNAKES
(Types)

BOA CONSTRICTOR	Female energy constricting your speech.
COBRA	Look for the female partner in situation. An asset.
CORAL	Someone being sharp in relationship.
RATTLE	Rattle, shake up of some sort, movement, danger of some sort. Striking out at someone.
TURTLE	Protection, grounded, reminder to look ahead and enjoy the journey, persistence.
VENOM	You are being poisoned in some way, food allergies.

RODENTS

BAT	Night vision, a different seeing and acting person.
BEAVER	Good at blocking the flow.
CHIPMUNK	Holding your thoughts or words back / requesting that one speaks up for themselves instead of stuffing ones feelings back inside.
GUINEAPIG	Squealer.

HAMSTER	Playful, person goes in continual pattern not changing or seeing other avenues / paths to take.
GROUNDHOG	Earths whether watcher. Very grounded and in the present moment, has a feel for vibrations of all sorts.
PRAIRIE DOG	Nosey individual, quick to hide, nothing gets past them.
MOUSE	Small and quick action needs to take place, a need to be flexibility in the situation.
RAT	Strength, has power to persuade others to follow.
SQUIRREL	Need to do some gathering of some sort. Something is in store for you, skittish energy.
WEASEL	Can not be trusted.

CHAPTER 2
CLOTHING

BELT	Strap yourself in for what is coming your way. Someone is holding you up, supporting you.
BELT BUCKLE	Bucking or resisting someone who is supporting you.
BERMUDA SHORTS	Person is sitting on the fence, not ready to make a decision.

BOOTS
(Types)

COWBOY	In need of a good kick to move you forward.
RAIN	You may be sloshing around in situation. Someone is all wet in their thinking.
WORK	You are protected, do your work, keep moving forward.
CUFFLINKS	A pair of something that links in some way to hold a situation firmly in alignment.
CUMBERBUND	A binding agreement that will be difficult to get out of.
DRESS SLACKS	Person walks their talk.
DRESS SHIRT	Person being assured of self or, decision made.

EVENING GOWN	Knows own worth. Showing you the dark side or contrast of situation.
GLOVES	Being given many different options.
JEANS	Getting down to the basics.
MU MU	Look for what is underneath the issue at hand, look at the bigger picture.
RAIN COAT	Protection.
ROBES	Feeling good and warm about situation or people.
SCARF	Wrapping things up.

SHOES
(Types)

CLOSED TOE	Closed minded, things are tight.
FLIP FLOPS	Can not make up ones mind, fence sitter, person enjoys being heard, likes to show both sides of situation.
HIGHHEELS	Needs grounding, persons head up in the clouds, scattered energy, concentrates on balance issue.
SANDLES	Open mindedness. welcomes fresh new thoughts.
SLIPS	(D) Making of poor judgment, falls back.
SMOKING JACKET	Your vision is cloudy.

SOCKS
(Types)

ANKLE	Binding, regarding something short.
CONTROL TOP NYLONS	Someone at the top has tight control.
CREW	More than one is working at this time.
DRESS	Assured of ones self.
KNEE HIGHS	Use as a measure of completion in situation.
SUPPORT HOSE	You are being showered with support at this time.

SUIT — You are suited to be doing what you are doing. You have all the tools to complete tasks.

SUNDRESS — Bright, joy and happiness.

SWEATERS
(Types) — Note the color and the texture of the sweater to gain more information.

BUTTON UP	Something is a little to exposed. Cover it up.
PULL OVER	Complete, now just bring it to completion.
ZIPPER	Just listen, keep it to yourself. Be quiet.

SWIMMING SUIT	Protected and in the flow.

TUXEDO	Dress up, pad, and embellish the situation or Thing. Formalize it.

UNDERWARE
(Types)

    BIKINI	Something or someone needs to be exposed and brought out at this time.

    BOXERS	(D) Fight for what is truth.

CHAPTER 3
EQUIPMENT, TOOLS & THINGS WITH WHEELS

AIRPLANE	Check the Type of plane, carries a large number, just a few passengers, a jet, fast moving etc. to answer your question.
AMBULANCE	Assistance needed quickly.
AUGER	Clean out of old unwanted energy.
BACKHOE	Bringing up old past lives stuff, things that are no longer serving you. Releasing of the old.
BBQ	The heating up of something or someone. Hot emotions, someone being drug over the coals.
BICYCLE	(D) Either 2 people are going shifts in their lives, or someone has just transformed to the second level, just changed gears.
BULLDOZER	Strong movement is required here, no more procrastination , just do it!!!!!!!
BUS	The movement of many thoughts, not buckled down as yet. creative mode.

CARS
(Types)

CAPTAIN (Fire)	In charge of putting out the office fires.

DRAGSTER	(D) A female figure being dragged into situation against her will.
FUNNY CAR	(D) Laughing at someone driving you endlessly around and around in circles.
PACE CAR	Findings one tempo, yoke, energy level.
POLICE	Ying Yang issue.
RACE	In a hurry to get things done.
SEDAN	Basics. Safe way to go with many exits.
SPORT	Weaving in and out of situation, energy and person lets no grass grow up their feet.
CRANE	Visionary, lifts most peoples spirits. May have their head in the clouds a lot. They deliver.
DOLLY	Carries a lot of weight on their shoulders.
DUMPSTER	(D) someone or something is being the dumping ground of Negative Energy.
EDGER	Person who is very assured of ones self, sharp dresser, detail person.
FLASH LIGHT	Sheds a little light on a subject. Watch for a news flash, bright idea.
GATE	Never makes ups ones mind. A swing voter Type. Check to see personality is gate open or closed minded.

GENERATOR	Motivator, a light bearer, person who starts things in motion.
HAMMER	Someone who is pounding in a point.
HELICOPTER	Someone has a thought that will rescue person, situation, lift ones spirits.
HORSE TRAILER	Carries a lot of wisdom, willing to work.
MOTORCYCLE	All about you on the tack of life, finding your balance.
PICK	A person who continually picks at situation it will never be right, picks on a person not letting up.
PLIERS	A handy person, likes to see whole picture. Grasps on to things quickly.
RAKE	A gatherer, combines things piled up, eager to release what is not serving them.
ROLLER-SKATES	Finding the simplest way to keep on rolling along and be balanced.
RV	Feeling comfortable getting your point across, can face many obstacles.
SAW	Cut ups, seeing joy, the need to release and laugh.
SERVING CART	Multiple ways to help out.
SCREWDRIVER	Listen up. Someone is forcing their will on you, driving in of a point made, someone is messing around with you.

SLIDING GLASS DOOR	Being able to see clearly the bigger picture.
SKATEBOARD	Being able to move forward with ease and flexibility.
SHOVEL	(D) Digging deep, moving things around.
SOCKET	Little ways of fine tuning or tweaking something.
TRAILER	(D) Follow the females lead.
TRAIN	Watch your step, the road my be bumpy. See what part of the train you are dealing with.
TROWEL	Spreading yourself to thin, level out.

TRUCKS
(Types) — Keep on moving forward. You can do it.

CEMENT	Look at core issue, what is the intention. Delivery presentation, receiving something, gift.
DUMP	(D) You are being dumped on, not your stuff. Everything downloaded at once.
EIGHTEEN WHEELER	Strong support in moving forward.
FIRE TRUCK	Sign of burning desire, put out the little fires in the situation.
GARBAGE	A need to clean out clutter.

PICK UP	Hauling around of stuff, picking up of something or someone.
EXTENDED CAB	Can be taken further. Stretch yourself or time a little further.
TRICYCLE	Keep plugging a long, try harder.
TRIMMER	Detail person, keep it neat.
WALKER	You are being supported in your step forward. Slow but deliberate.
WHEEL-BARROW	One person is carrying a heavy load.
WHEELCHAIR	Seeing things on the middle level, a seated view position.
WRENCH	A disturbance of some kind.

CHAPTER 4
FOOD AND BEVERAGES

BEEF
(Types)

    HAMBURGER   Plain and simple.

    RIBS   Not much to go on making a decision.

    ROAST   Taking a lot of criticism.

    STEAK   One has a lot of time or money invested.

CASSEROLE   A lot of variables or components to this project.

CHEESE   Happy and smiling, lighten up and find joy.

DESSERT   Completion and celebration time, ending.

CAKES
(Types)   Rich, effortless.

    CHEESECAKE   A sweet deal, effortless.

    LAYER   Peeling away of levels no longer serving you. The filling up of good things, a way of measuring where you are now and how much further before completion.

Sue Chandler

CANDY
(Types)

	BAR	The information is sweet and has a limited time before completion.
	BOX	Look for the variety of nice things you can sink your teeth into.
	LOLLIPOP	Project or situation has a slow methodical pace. There will be completion, and ending.
ICE CREAM		Something piled onto the main issue or situation.
ALA MODE		Chill out.
ICE CREAM CONES		(D) Cold thoughts, yelling for your attention. Thoughts are contained.
ICE CREAM FLOATS		(D) Cold Negative thoughts still floating around.
ICE CREAM SODA		Cold thoughts still there, it has not changed.
ICE CEAM SUNDAE		Cold negative thoughts are piling up.

ICE CREAM
(Types)

	CHOCOLATE	Something is grounded (D) the written document is late.
	CHOCOLATE CHIP	Partially grounded. (See above)

CHOCOLATE CHIP MINT		Grounded most of the time.(See above). Rich and or expensive.
NEAPOLITAN		Person can see more than one side of situation.
STRAWBERRY		(D) Takes small sips of situation, very narrow minded.
VANILLA		Pure thought.

SHERBETS
(Types) — (D) you can count on having the correct answer.

ORANGE	Relationship a sure thing. Like the sunset.
PINEAPPLE	Powerful, visionary, sees from the very beginning of situation through to the end.
RAINBOW	Bright and colorful in all ways, balance, joy and happiness is sheds light on the situation.
RASPBERRY	You have been burned or hurt in some way.

PIES
(Types) — Things are equally divided.

APPLE	Start at the beginning, take each step at a time.

	BANANA CREAM	Facts are contained in one place, start at top.
	BERRY	Tart or bitter sweet.
	CHERRY	(D) Situation is the pits, usually comes in twos.
	CHOCOLATE CREAM	Top person is grounded yet needs to communicate or there will be a delay.
	COCONUT CREAM	Person in charge is hard shelled or headed.
	CUSTARD	Independent spirit, does their own thing.
	KEY LIME	Person feels only their ideas are the best, they have the key idea that opens the doors for success.
	LEMON MERINGUE	Balanced situation, may be a little bitter sweet, remain optimistic.
	MINCEMEAT	(D) Dissected core things in situation. The main substance has been gone over.
	PECAN	Small amount of something is contained.
	PUMPKIN	(D) Family if pumped up.

FRUIT
(Types)

    APPLE   (See above pies)

BANANA	(See above pies)
BERRIES	(See above pies)
GRAPES	Bunches of choices.
KIWI	(D) More than one person has the answer.
MELON	Refreshing thoughts.
TOMATO	Two people walking forward together.
LAMB CHOP	Gentle speaking.

PORK
(Types)

BACON	Cutting things rather thin, things stacking up.
CHOP	Chopping of some sort, removing excess of something, being hit in the face.
HAM	Finding some humor, laugh it is healthy.
RIBS	Getting down to the bare or core issues.
ROAST	Burning of some sort, or bad mouthing.

POULTRY
(Types)

CHICKEN	Scared, exposed of some sort.

GAME HEN	Female energy ready to join you and play.
PHEASANT	(D) Pleasant.
TURKEY	Stuffed with all the information you need.

SPREADS & SPICES
(Types)

CATSUP	Need to catch up on something or an aspect of life one needs to address.
GARLIC	Something is strong and may be overpowering in nature.
HORSERADISH	A good cleansing should take place.
HOT SAUCE	Dealing with hot and spicy issue.
MAYONNAISE	Pure rich thought evenly spread around.
MUSTARD	Power is slow and low.
ONION FLAKES	Little emotions. Scattered energy.
PARSLEY	The little extras used will make appearance attractive and successful.
SALT & PEPPER	Balanced couple.
STEAK SAUCE	Meat of situation is being covered up in some way.
SUGAR	Something sweet, raw or refined.

VEGETABLES
(Types)

ASPARAGUS	Person thin yet stocky.
BEANS	Strong, powerful.
BROCCOLI	Bunches of good healthy, filtering out bad cells.
CORN	Corny, Crazy, multi-faceted, very organized.
PEAS	Group of people on same wave length.
SQUASH	(D) Put down of some kind.

CHAPTER 5
GAMES (ALL TYPES)

BOARD GAMES

BACKGAMMON	Deliberate moves, pairing up of some kind.
CANDYLAND	(D) Sweet place to be or live.
CHECKERS	A move is going to take place. (Double jump is home location and work).
CHESS	The gentleman needs to be honored and appreciated by younger souls.
CLUE	Finding a piece of the bigger picture.
CRIBBAGE	(D) A person who is acting baby like, someone carrying a lot of old baggage.
MONOPOLY	Group speaks, no room for individual thought, power plays, high rollers.
OPERATION	Things need to be stitched up, something is leaking out.
SHOOTS & LADDERS	New growth, a way to reach higher for end results, time to step up to the plate and make something happen.

CARD GAMES

BLACK JACK (21)	You are taking a risk, being given several tries to add to situation, now legal age.
BRIDGE	Connection between two of something.

CANASTA	Given chances to attain clarity.
CONCENTRATION	Think about it, be focused.
FAN TAN	Situation to hot, a need to cool down a bit.
GIN RUMMY	Giddy, not grounded, happy, light headed.
GO FISH	Need to take time to relax.
HEARTS	Remember many love you.
KINGS CORNER	No matter which way you go, authority rules.
OLD MAID	Older female, wisdom, clean up.
PINOCHLE	Only seeing one side or situation.
SLAP JACK	Wake up to what is happening right in front of you.
SNAP	Instant awakening, get with the program, get moving, quick decisions.
SOLITAIRE	Confined to the rules, by ones self.
SPADES	Dig deeper, find the light.
UNO	Number one.
WAR	Unrest, bickering, arguments.

CASINO GAMES

BINGO	Attaining and lining up of something. Right on the spot.
BACCARAT	(D) You are being stretched, like your back is on a rack.
CARIBBEAN STUD	A tan handsome male. Kissed by the sun.
CRAPS	Taking a risk. Results are not as favorable.
DEALER	Be cautious what is being offered, all the cards are not yet revealed.
HORSE RACE	Racing to finish something up, completion stop messing around, get moving, just get ready and GO.
KENO	You know, you own the key to make it happen.
POKER	(D) Someone poking at or trying to get female's attention, making fun of, straight face.
TEXAS HOLD THEM	Takes a big amount of energy to contain what you have & what you are dealing with.
THREE CARD	(D) This indicates three in some way.
VIDEO	Documentation, affirmation.
ROULETTE	Many options, different ways to accomplish same goal.

Just Ask

SLOT MACHINE	An indicator or completion. From Penny Machines, shiny new beginnings to $5.00 machine indicate completion, Jack Pot.

CHILDREN'S GAMES

DICE	An indicator of amount of something.
DOMINOS	A rapid collapse of something. Duplication is involved.
DUCK, DUCK, GOOSE	The going around and around about something, circling, no more evading something for you might get caught.
DODGE BALL	Evading the situation, or you might get hit with something more, be willing to be flexible. And open minded.
FOUR SQUARE	Four equals of some sort.
LO NDON BRIDGE	Proper steps are being taken to bring something together, connecting.
MARBLES	Contained space. Being viewed, watch out what is coming from all sides.
MUSICAL CHAIRS	Keeping up the pace, fighting for your part in something, finding relief at times, listen to the tone of project.
PICK UP STICKS	Everything is colorfully placed before you, now gently work on each piece.
PIN THE TAIL ON THE DONKEY	Being blind, things going around and around but take a stab at it or chance it.

Sue Chandler

ROCK, SCISSORS, PAPER	Sometimes you get covered up, sometimes squashed and sometimes cut up. See if the risk is worth it to you.
RED ROVER	Come over to the other side to see what they may offer.
RING AROUND THE ROSIES	Something appears good yet will fall or will leave or abandon you at the end.
SIMON SAYS	Someone following the leader and you are being tested to bee if you are awake and focused because if not you will be reprogrammed with someone else's thoughts.
TAG	It is all about you. You are the one, no one else, you are it.
TETHER BALL	Someone or something is getting beat up.

CHAPTER 6
ITEMS FOUND IN HOME

BATHROOM AREA

BATHTUB	The cleansing of something and a way to release that which is no longer wanted.
EYE SHADOW	Not seeing clearly, the situation may be a little out of focus, shadows. A way to accentuate something.
MEDICINE CHEST	A place to go to get help & fix something.
MIRROR	To view the entire picture, to see self.
SHOWER CAP	Your thoughts are protected.
SHOWER CURTAIN	Whatever you are doing can not be seen.
SHOWER HEAD	Beating in a point or clear thought.

BEDROOM

ALARM CLOCK	Time to wake up to something.
BEDS	Check to see the size of the bed, describing the size of that which you are dealing with.
DRESSER	Container, (D) define the energy the female is wearing.
DUST RUFFLE	Frills around situation.

HANGER	Hang in there, things are looking great.
PILLOW	Fluffy cloud like feeling.
PILLOW SHAM	(D) Taking of medicine, getting a raw deal regarding something.
MAKE UP TABLE	Something or someone is being made up, things are looking good.
MATTRESS PAD	Comfortable place to be.
PICTURE	Being able to see everything all at once.
RUG	Watch that it is not being pulled out from under you, the covering up of something.
SHEETS	Covering something up, feeling snug and secure.

DEN/STUDY

CD'S	Verbal validation.
CHAIR	Being comfortable and in alignment.
CLOCK	Move on. Also an indication of a certain length of time, documentation of duration event took place. Linier time measurement.
COMPUTER	Brain has the information needed.(D) You got it.
MOUSE	Knows how to get into things effortlessly. Be flexible.

SCREEN	Showing you the larger picture. Your life is running or being shown.
TOWER	Tells you how high you are with regarding something. So high it may crash.
COPIER	Being duplicated in some way.
COUCH	Place to take a breather.
DESK	A need to get working.
DVD	Audio and visual documentation.
FAX MACHINE	Clairvoyance, sending a visual item from a distance.
MAP	Direction of your path.
REAMS OF PAPER	(D) Lots of documentation of work completed.
TELEVISION	A way of viewing the larger picture.
THROW RUG	(D) Discarding that what which was once covered under the rug.

EXERCISE ROOM

BALANCE BEAM	Walking a thin line.
BENCH PRESS	Pressing or moving forward.
CHANGING ROOM	(D) There is room for change.

DUMB BELLS	Ringing, getting your attention to see what appears to be information being given you, there is more then one way.
EXERCISE BALLS	Exercise your right to see all sides of situation.
GLOVES	Examine all the different parts of view. You are a fine catch.
JACUZZI	Being comfortable with the flow moving quickly.
MATS	A blanket protection.
PERSONAL TRAINER	Your individual teacher or guide.
REBOUNDER	Bouncing back in a small way from a situation.
TRAMPOLINE	Jumping high above situation. (D) Poor person of need some help.
PROTEIN BAR	The need for more energy.
RINGS	Going full circle. Coming around.
ROWING MACHINE	Moving forward at ones own pace.
SCALE	Finding balance. What is the number on scale, it is giving you a number or a way to evaluate what you are asking for.
SAUNA	Soak, stay still and relax, just be.

STEAM ROOM	Something has a lot of hot energy around it, there is room or need to cool down.
STEPS	Movement of some sort. (Check the number of steps you have been taking.)
TOWEL	Wiping up a mess. Soaking up information.
TREADMILL	Moving slowly at first, when comfortable, moving quickly.
UN-EVEN BARS	There is no balance or equality here.
VAULT	Things are safe and being uplifted.
WALL CLIMBING	Hanging in there, you are almost at the top.
WEIGHTS	Added heaviness. (Check out the number to get how much change needs to be lost or gained.)

KITCHEN AREA

APPLE CORER	What is the core issue?
BAKING DISH	Something in progress. Warming up (Check to see the temperature and how long it needs until completion.)
BLENDER	Purging of information.

BOWL	Depending on the size of bowl, example large, contains a lot of information. Bowls used to mix all aspects of situation, if bowls are ceramic, it is solid or permanent, if plastic, it can be discarded.
CAN GOODS	Look for the good in the matter.
CAN OPENER	It is safe to open up to others. (D) female can be read like a book.
CLEANERS	The cleansing of the situation.
CLOCKS	It is time. (Check the number it has meaning.)
COFFEE POT	Time to get up and start moving.
COOKBOOK	Detailed instructions on what is being prepared.
COOKIE SHEET	Things are being laid out for you to see.
COOKING UTENSILS	Different tools are being shown to get best results.
COUNTER	Other offers being made. (D) a way of measurement.
DETERGENT	A need to clean up situation, there were bumps in the road that are now resolved.
DISHES	You have been fed what you need for success. (D) remove the male energy.
DISH TOWEL	A clean up, mopped up the mess.

Just Ask

DISHWASHER	A way to clean up many issues at once.
DRAINER	(D) The releasing of female energy.
FREEZER	No movement. (D) Female set free.
GARBAGE DISPOSAL	The getting rid of something old.
GLASSES	You are able to see the clarity of something.
IRON	A need to smooth things out, a situation has some wrinkles or blockages in it.
JUICER	Give female a squeeze or some loving.
KNIFE BLOCK	Holder of all the sharp tools used in life.
LADLE	A large scoop of something.
LEFT OVER CONTAINER	A place that keeps that which has not been used to date.
MICROWAVE	Quick solution.
NAPKINS	Let up on your family.
OVEN	A heated situation or person.
PLACEMATS	Setting of boundaries.
PLATTER	You are in the process of handling a lot of different things at once, larger than your normal work load.
POTATO PEELER	Situation is still on the ground, getting around to a fresh new start.

POTS & PANS	Different ways of preparing something.
POT HOLDER	Keeping the contents of something safe and ready to move.
REFRIGERATOR	Storing large amounts of things until ready for consumption of some kind.
SILVERWARE	Tools or ones gifts to serve with.
SINK	(D) Something is falling down quickly.
SPATULA	Looking at something that is flattened, flipped, need to turn something over, to look at both sides of a situation, one side might already be completed.
SPONGE	Sopping up the spillage of some kind.
STOVE	Being able to have more than one project going at once. Two may be on the back burner.
TABLECLOTH	The covering up of some kind.
TEA POT	Pretty way of containing steam.
TRIVET	Small cover up.

LAUNDRY ROOM

BLEACH	The purifying of something.
BROOM	The making of a clean sweep.
CLOTHES BASKET	A place for everything.

DRYER	Something needs to be given a fresh start and new air placed under it. Old stuff be filtered out and cleansed.
DUSTERS	(D) Outdated things released from Female.
DUST PAN	Scooping up of old out clutter no longer needed.
FOLDING TABLE	A place to spread out and organize things.
LIQUID LAUNDRY SOAP	The pouring on of someone else's will to clean up their act.
FABRIC SOFTENER	Lighten up the situation.
STAIN REMOVER	Removal of unfavorable markings.
VENTS	The need to remove angry energy.
WASHING MACHINE	Time to clean up something in big way.
WAX	You are shining, all a glow, someone is buffed, large muscles.

PLAY ROOM / FAMILY ROOM

BLOCKS	The building of a basic structure.
BOOK CASES	Holders of knowledge and wisdom.
BOOKS	Tools created by a teacher.

Sue Chandler

BUILDING SET	Ultimate creating of a creation.
CARS	(See Chapter 3)
CDs	(See above in Dens)
DRESS UP OUTFITS	Fully equipped and outfitted with all new things.
DOLLS	Nurturing, playing with that which is pretend. (D) Beautiful.
GAMES	Who might not be truthful with you at this time.
HATS	Doing many jobs at once.
PLAY KITCHEN	Playing and making a mock up of real thing.
RACE CAR RUG	Mapping out what is happening, seeing the bigger picture.
TABLE & CHAIRS	A comfortable match to digest what is happening at this time.
TRAIN SET	You are on tack, following your path and you equipped with all the tools necessary to make it a success.

CHAPTER 7
NATURE

AIR	Fresh breath.
ANIMALS WILD	Untamed exciting energy. Male and female energy.
BOATING	Being able to drift aimlessly, not grounded.
BABBLING BROOK	Someone keeps talking on and on.
CAMPING	Going back to basics in a natural way.
CLOUDS	Formations not being able to see the beside them.
CREEK	A little movement is taking place.
CRYSTAL	Being able to see clearly.
DIRT	Relating to earth energy. Ground great for planting of new ideas.
EARTH	A place we grow.
EARTHQUAKE	Get a moving. Shake up of some form.
FAULT	Weakest point of something.
FISHING	Searching for something.
FLOWER	Something colorful is opening up. (Check to see how far it has opened for a time reference.)

GRASS	(Green) new growth (Yellow) something is dying out, measurement of height of the grass.
HIKING	Take a walk to cool down, or take a hike, get out of situation. Going up to get answers.
HURRICANE	Kundalini energy stirring up something and putting it elsewhere.
LAKE	Body of water, check out the waters. Movement as a possible answer.
LIGHTENING	You are being struck, movement needed.
MINERALS	Dig deep to get the real value.
MOON	Your night light. (Check the size as a way to measure.)
MOUNTAIN	The view at the top, visionary, look us to see your goal. You are close to reaching the top.
OCEAN	The example of being in a massive amount of powerful energy, being in the flow of life.
RAIN	A cleansing on some level, drifting along going with the flow, a down stream thought, relinquishing control.
ROCK	You have a solid foundation.
STARS	Your guidance system, source of light.
STORM	Disturbing energy, anger.

STREAM	In the flow, a trickle of information coming in.
SUN	A God Type energy. Something is heating up.
TORNADO	A need to settle down. Moving rapidly and missing the joy full journey.
TRAIL	Looking at your lives path. Ways to follow, choices.
TREES	The root of the situation and showing its growth of the matter.

CHAPTER 8
PEOPLE AND OCCUPATIONS

ACROBAT	Someone or thing flying high.
ACTOR/ACTRESS	The playing out of male and female. energy. Giving a way of interpreting situation.
AGENT	Representation of something or someone.
ANIMAL TRAINER	Teacher of the beasts on the planet.
ANNOUNCER	Describes and verbalizes action taking place.
ARTIST	Interprets, A Way, in which something is viewed, an expression of self.
ATTENDANT	Keeps thing in proper place. Attends to situation.
ATTORNEY	Looking at your journey and acting on it.
AUNT	A smaller version of a parent figure.
AUTHOR	A teacher of thoughts and words.
BAKER	Starts and completes things, use to rising and falling, creator.
BASEBALL PLAYER	Might be a need catch and idea and run with it.

BASKETBALL PLAYER	Always attempting to be correct and score.
BACHELOR	Doing things alone. Male energy looking for a batch or bunch of female energy.
BAIL BONDSMAN	Helps one out of a tight bind or is in bondage.
BALLERINA	Keep high beautiful thought. Keeps on ones toes.
BAND LEADER	A person knowing all of the aspects of situation.
BARTENDER	Constantly mixing or blending things up or together.
BEE KEEPER	Keeps tract of the sweet things in life.
BEAUTICIAN	Always looking to improve or beautify someone or something.
BUS BOY	Able to keep things picked and cleaned up.
BUTCHER	Separates that which is of higher and lower grades of something, a cut up.
BOXER	The keeping of rage in a small container. The storing up of female energy.
CAPTAIN	In charge, knows and uses limits and boundaries.
CARDIOLOGIST	Knows the tempo or the beat of the heart of the matter.

CARPENTER	Basic builder from ground up.
CARPET LAYER	Smart, knows how to cover something up.
CLOWN	Master of disguise. Sees the happy side of situation. Encourages laughter.
CLERK	Record keeper.
COACH	Major teacher.
COMEDIAN	Can find humor in any situation.
CONSTRUCTION WORKER	Builds things, reader of the grids or maps.
COMPUTER TECH	Analyzes & fine tuning of project. Detail person.
CRANE OPERATER	Operates on a higher level, quick to make decisions.
COUSINS	Not the highest on the list of details at hand. Makes decisions just because, not understanding why.
CUSTODIAN	Clean sweeps things.
DANCER	Creativity in movement.
DESIGNER	Creative, comes up with different ways to present the same thing, reads the signs.
DELIVERY PERSON	Person can be counted on to bring what is needed.
DETECTIVE	Sneaky energy, secretive.

Just Ask

DENTIST	Fills the hole in the situation allowing one to take a big bite out of the situation.
DIETITIAN	Works with all aspects of big picture.
EDITOR	Person is able to make changes for the betterment of a situation. Sees entire scope.
ELECTRICIAN	Energy worker, understands how something functions and is wired.
ENGINEER	One who is the mover of the larger picture.
FACE PAINTER	Is able to temporarily change the energy or mood of situation by creating a change.
FARMER	Deals with mother nature, planter of the seeds of life. Reaps and sows.
FATHER	Master of things and beings.
FIREMAN	Person who deals with the heat of the matter.
FLORIST	Makes things pretty and uses color.
GARDENER	Weed out things dead things, out and replants the new.
GOVERNOR	Appointed to over see project or people.
GRANDPARENT	Wisdom with age. Neutering teacher of family.
GROCER	Supplier of the nutrients of that at hand.

HERO	Someone raising to the occasion at hand and taking action on it.
HOBO/ TRAMP	Left to defend for ones self.
LIBRARIAN	Keeper of the book of knowledge.
LOBBYIST	Insisting on keeping outside the box of something.
ILLUSTRATOR	Can draw and present a situation using Their interpretation.
JEWELER	Always looking for the gem of the situation.
JOURNALIST	Interoperates and reports a belief system.
JUDGE	Places a view point on you, someone else's belief system, not necessarily yours.
JURY	A judgment given to a situation or person.
LAWYER	Defender of some established belief system.
MAID	(D) Winner, got it made.
MAKE UP ARTIST	Creator of color by design.
MASSAGE THERAPIST	Clearing of emotions blockages of all Types and on all levels.
METEOROLOGIST	Can weather any situation.
MINISTER	The giver of little bits of information.

MODEL	A Way to interpret a reality to come.
MORTICIAN	Still working with something that no longer has any life to it. Dead issue.
MOTHER	The one who gives life and birth to all things. Nurturer.
MUSICIAN	Knows the tones of life.
NEPHEW	Younger male energy.
NIECE	Younger female energy.
NURSE	Caretaker, nurturer, feeds.
PARAMEDIC	With speed, takes care of situation and persons involved.
PEDIATRICIAN	Walks with the little ones on the planet.
PHOTOGRAPHER	Documents events. Sees.
PHYSICIAN	Works on the physical, healer.
POLICE	(D) Sticks to the cold hard facts, enforces situations.
PRESIDENT	Leader of situation.
PSYCHOLOGIST	Working on different or abnormal people or things unable to fit in somewhere in a logical manner.
PILOTS	The first ones to try and test something.
PLUMBER	Cleans out the dirty stuff that stinks and has blocked everything up.

PRINCIPAL	The leading point of situation.
RACECAR DRIVER	Fast moving decision maker.
RECEPTIONIST	Clairaudient, takes note of what is needed to be heard or documented.
REFEREE	Puts out fires before they get heated up.
SAILOR	Go with her decision.
SALES	Tries to meet ones needs, (D) goes where the wind blows.
SCULPTURE	Forms a clear way to look at things. Molds things.
SEAMSTRESS	Tries to make even that which caused Stress.
SECRETARY	Multi-tasker, taking notes of the event.
STEWARDESS	Female energy server, releases stress.
STOCK PERSON	Keeping stock or track of situation.
SURGEON	(D) Keeps things in order, keeps thing moving forward.
TEACHER	Holder of wisdom.
TIMEKEEPER	Watches the duration of event and sets boundaries.
TRAVEL AGENT	Introduces many ways to get to ending of destination of some kind.
TRUCK DRIVER	Keeps driving the point in.

UMPIRE	Keeps reaching for the higher picture.
UNCLE	Another male energy to follow.
VICE PRESIDENT	Follows leader's actions, things appear to be in a tight squeeze.
VOCALIST	Speaks one truth, singing ones praises.
WAITRESS	Stop, a women is taking care of it.

CHAPTER 9
SIGNS

ADD SIGN	Extra is being given to you.
BACKSPACE	You have gone to far, bake up a little.
CAP LOCK	The person has everything under their control, no chance for change here. You have not been given the entire
CAUTION	Be aware. (D) wake up the crow is letting you know what is happening, listen.
CAUTION WET	Be aware of the slippery situation.
COMA	Pause and take a deep breath.
CURVES AHEAD	Something needs to be straightened
DELETE	Something needs to be eliminated or erased.
DISABLED	Not wanting to move forward.
DOCKING	Pulling over for a rest.
DOWN ARROW	Situation is going down.
DRUG FREE ZONE	Safe place to proceed.
END	Completion of some sort.
ENTER	The time is right to make a forward move.
EQUAL SIGN	The same. Side by side.

EXCLAMATION MARK	Making your point about something.
FLAMMABLE	Warning, something is ready to ignite and take off.
FORWARD	A direction of movement taking place towards that which is in front of you.
HOME	Beginning comfortable, familiar place.
INSERT	An addition to your existing piece of information.
ITALICS	Highlighting said information.
LOADING ZONE	A designated place to add something to existing material.
OFF	Shut down. No longer operational.
ON	Up and running.
MERGING	Placing together of more than one of something.
ONE WAY	Something heading in only one direction. No deviating.
PAGE DOWN	Downward motion, being called.
PAGE UP	Upward motion.
PEDESTRIAN CROSSING	Safe place being between the lines.
PERCENTAGE	Only a certain amount is designated for something.

QUESTION MARK	Take time to review the contents of the materials authenticity in question, wonderment.
NO ADMISSION	You have just been stopped in some way.
NO PASSSING	Have to stay right where you are at this point.
NO SMOKING	Only clarity allowed, no clouding the issues at hand.
NUMBER SIGN	Describing a set amount of something.
MINUS SIGN	Something is being taken away, check to see if it is for your highest good.
RESTRICTED AREA	Only certain facts are being shown you at this time, other parts or areas to be worked on now.
RESTROOM	(D) A place to rest for a time.
SCHOOL BUS STOP	A place to stop and learn a lot.
SHIFT	Something has changed, moved growth has taken place, shift happens.
SLIDE AREA	Unstable footing, something or one is falling down or moving.
SLOW	Lessen the speed being taken.
SPEED LIMIT	Look at the number on this sign. (An indicator of time, or amount.) Boundaries are set in place here.
STOP	Come to a complete halt.

STOP SIGNALS	A message is being given. (Indicator Red stop, Yellow be cautious, Green go.)
STREET NUMBER	Giving location of something.
TRAIN CROSSING	Be aware, something is coming in fast and is in alignment.
WATCH YOUR STEP	Look at where you are stepping or placing something.
WARNING	You have been put on notice.
YIELD	Slow down a bit to observe what might be coming your way, check your surroundings.

CHAPTER 10
SPORTS (ALL TYPES)

BASEBALL

ANNOUNCER	Narrating even or situation.
BASES	Measure how far along one is regarding Situation.
BASEBALL CAMP	Group effort.
BAT	You have the tools needed for a hit.
BATTING PRACTICE	Need to take more time to review, and repeat over again what is needed.
BATTER UP	Now it is your turn.
BLEACHER SEATS	Less expensive, not having much worth.
BOBBLE HEAD	Not grounded, going back in forth with decisions, nod of approval.
BOX SEATS	Has a good eye regarding the larger situation,. tight boundaries are in place.
BUNT	Having to run up to face a change.
CAMERA	Documenting action that has taken place.
CHALK	Temporary boundaries, a way to communicate using words or pictures.
CHANGE UP	You are being thrown something different then being used at this time.

COACH	Demonstrating knowledge.
CONDITIONING	Staying on tract with regiment, exercising your rights about something.
CURVE BALL	Watch out, something different is being thrown your way.
DIAMOND	A rich work sight, something or someone is precious.
DOUBLE PLAY	Being able to do two things at once.
DUG OUT	Some way the situation has been saved.
FANS	You are being supported by many, the need to cool down.
FAST PITCH	Move a little quicker to accomplish task at hand, speed up.
FLY BALL	Look up to see what is coming.
GLOVE OR MITT	Catching up on something, regaining control.
GROUNDBALL	Having time to make your move.
HOME PLATE	Completion, you have scored the big one.
KNUCKLEBALL	Something is wearing you down.
LINE DRIVE	Right on the mark, being in alignment.
MOUND	Raising of the stakes, higher then others.

NATIONAL ANTHEM	Commitment to ones beliefs, the singing of praises.
ON DECK CIRCLE	Getting ready to strut your stuff.
ORGAN	Making nice music, having rhythm.

POSITIONS
(Types)

CATCHER	(D) Catch her, female energy.
CENTER FIELDER	Center field, look right in the middle.
DESIGNATED HITTER	Bringing in the big guns.
LEFT FIELDER	Something is way out there.
PITCHER	(D) Release the female.
RIGHT FIELDER	(D) Scattered energy, a need for grounding.
OUTFIELDER	Not paying attention to details, off balance.
SHORT STOP	(D) Stop for a short time, take a break.

RAKE	Filtering out that which does or dose not serve you. Cleaning up.
SEVENTH INNING STRETCH	A time to relax a little, taking a breather.
SLIDE	Coming in low not to be seen, just making the deadline.

SCOREBOARD	Seeing where you stand in overall situation.
STEALING THE BASE	Taking a risk of being caught.
STRIKE	Swinging out at someone or something.
TEAM	More than one working together
UMPIRE	Authority figure calling the shots.
VENDORS	Someone eager to sell you their goods or ideas.
WALK	Slow your pace down, you might want to be an observer.
WORLD SERIES	Seeing things on a Global level.

BASKETBALL

BACKBOARD	Something or someone to bounce off of.
BACKCOURT	The issue is in the back ground position.
BASELINE	Boundaries have been set.
BASKET	The holding of an objective.
CENTER CIRCLE	Right in the middle, perfect alignment; Great view of entire picture.
COURT	Look at the area in which you are playing or creating to see if it is large enough, is it reaching the right people?

DRIBBLING	Releasing a certain amount of something.
DUNK	Something is being looked at, cleansed and looked at once again.
ELBOWING	Someone is pushing you out of the way.
FLOOR	Someone is walking all over you.
FORWARDS	Advancing, movement towards your dreams.
FOUL LINE	Exhibiting unsafe practices, crossing the boundaries.
FREE THROW LINE	Unexpected miracle, a chance for advancement.
JUMP BALL	Who's time to take over the project?. The highest bid wins.
LAY UP	You are being fed information to help you out.
REBOUND	Had a bad wrap, coming back to start again.
SLAM DUNK	You made it happen without a doubt.
TIP OFF	You are receiving extra information for your advancement.
TRAVELING	Gathering information from other places.

BICYCLING

BIKE FRAME	Take a look at the basic frame work of the project at hand.
BREAKS	A need to slow down or stop.
CHAINS	Are you feeling bound up in someway? Check the links out, is one weaker or stronger? A need for balance in order to keep going.
GEARS	Check at what speed the event or situation moving and is an adjustment needed here?
HANDLEBAR	(D) Someone is having difficulty handling alcohol, jail confined, can not see any way out of situation.
KICKSTAND	(D) Stop standing around, get a move on.
MIRRORS	See what is right in front of you, reflection.
PEDALS	There is strength here in moving forward.
REFLECTORS	(D) A time to look back on what has taken place, the past, good time to evaluate and make the changes needed.
SEAT	(D) Sit down.
SHIFTER	(D) There is a shift taking place or there needs to be a women change to lead position, be in female energy.

SPOKES	Intertwining as a team to make something move, one thing out of alignment, a jamming will take place.
TUBES	Check the tires, are you loosing air or energy? Time to change something or add new life to an old situation.
TURN SIGNALS	Check to see if you need to go backwards (Left indicator) or forwards (Right indicator).
WHEELS	Moving in some direction, Check the wearing of the treads. Are you in balance and aligned with Source? Or are you spinning around in circles?

BOWLING

ALLEY	Location.
BACKUP	(D) Look at the work already completed, take a step back from the situation and be an observer.
BAGS	Contains what is needed.
BALL	Bouncing right along.
DIAMOND	A precise guide line.
FINGERTIP	A little lift in the situation at hand, someone upset with you.
FOUL LINE	Need to set boundaries, do not cross the line.

GUTTER	A place to hold clutter not needed.
HOOK	Going at something in an unconventional way.
LEAGUE	Perfect number that has gathered. Score.
SCORE BOARD	(D) Keeping track of progress.
SHOES	Protection in walking forward in situation.
SPARE	(D) An extra chance.
SPLIT	(D) A separation of some kind, a break up.
STICKUM	Hold on to what you already have. Stick to what you are working on.
STRIKE	Putting your mark on something, taking a negative hit.
TOURNAMENT	Check out what the goal is all about, what is the core issue, what is really meant to happen.
TOWEL	Getting rid of what is not needed wipe or clean appropriately.
TURKEY	Gratitude for the abundance, celebration with noise.

DANCE

	DANCE BALLET	Graceful, doing things on a high level. Keeping on top of things working with the Divine feminine energy.
	BALLROOM	(D) Things taking a long time to complete, sadness associated with situation at hand.
	BREAK A LEG	Anything can be accomplished, wishing good luck.
	COUPLES	Two working together.
	DUOS	Two persons required to perform task at hand.
	5,6,7,8	Alignment has just taken effect. Ready to start, go you have the green light to start.
	JIVE	Someone or something is moving quickly now.
	GLIDE	Just sailing along smoothly.
	HIP HOP	Younger vibration, anxious energy, hop to it.
	HULA	Someone in the middle of a situation is ready to slowly and deliberately move or shift things around.
	JAZZ	Excited about what is happening.

LEG WARMERS	Keep the project or person undercover for right now, things need to warm up a little before being exposed.
LIFTS	Raising up the tone of situation.
PIROUETTE	High Vibration, visionary, proud.
MENTAL FOCUS	Stay on track, be in the present moment, hone in on one thing.
MIRROR IMAGE	Look at what is going on around you. The same is happening to you as well.
MODERN DANCE	Creating ideas, using new energy.
SHOES	Magic, finding something that is exciting and creative while keeping moving, indicating the rhythm or tone of situation or person.
SLIDE	Downward motion, slipping out of alignment.
SOLO	Working alone, single.
SQUARE DANCING	Keeping up with a set routine. Partner matching your energy. Squaring up with something.
STAGE	Location for work to be completed. High performance.
SWING	Teaming up, going along with things, moving forward and taking a step back to be an observer of a situation or person.

TAKING A BOW		Flexibility, receiving your just reward of appreciation.
TAP		Keep up with the beat of the program, no slowing down,. wake up call.
TOE SHOES		Up high, good view of the situation pointing in the right direction.
TRIOS		Three required at this time.
TWIST		Be flexible in the situation, Little adjustments needed.
TWO STEP		Going around in order and facing the music. Look at what is right there in front of you.
THE JERK		Someone is not listening to reason, being difficult.

FISHING

FISHING BAIT	Going for the meat of something.
BOBBERS	Going up and down.
CASTING	Flinging it out there.
HAT	Protection at the top, a covering up.
HOOK	Once something or someone has you so to speak, it is difficult to escape.
FISHING VEST	Having all the right little nooks and crannies.

FLIES	(D) Something bothersome.
KNIFE	Something sharp.
LINE	(D) On the straight and narrow.
LURE	(D) Being brought into something, not always of your wanting.
MINNOW	A lot of little things going your way.
NET	Time to catch up on something.
REEL	Repeating something over and over.
ROD	Something is stiff and straight.
SARDINE	Alignment situation.
SCALE	How much weight are you giving the situation?
SINKER	Something is falling down, going to bottom.
TACKLE BOX	Attempting to master something.
TROLLING	Going along with it, being in the flow.
WADERS	Floating to the top.

FOOTBALL

BEER	Numbing of self, loss of consciousness.
CHAIN	A way to measure something, being punished of some sort.

CHEERLEADERS	You are being supported, being shown gratitude for that which you have done and will do.
CLEATS	Digging into the meat of the situation.
DEFENSE	Defending your actions.
DOWNS	Measuring aspects of time or space.
FIELD	A place to play and have some fun.
FIELD GOAL	The highest action taken and winning.
FOOTBALL	You are kicking something around that is inflated.
GOAL POST	Fitting something in between, attaining your dreams or purpose.
HELMET	All about protecting what is important.
PADS	Protecting the parts of a situation.
QUARTERBACK	(D) 25 percent of the action. returned.
REFEREE	Seeing that everything is fare, the visionary.
SIDELINE	Boundaries, spectators , observing not the main players.
TOUCH DOWN	Scoring and doing the best you can be and being rewarded.

GOLF

BAG	A way in which to keep all things together so to make better choices.
BALL	Little things are rolling along.
CHIPPING	Taking a small piece at a time.
CLUBHOUSE	The gathering center, time to start and finish.
CLUB	Showing strength, power, how far one will drive in the point,
CUP	Holding of important object, completion.
DRIVER	Powerfully moving your intent forward.
EAGLE	Performing in the highest fashion. someone is flying high.
FOLLOW THROUGH	Making sure you continue on the right track.
GLOVES	Catching the movement, protection.
GRIP	Holding on tightly to what you are working on or want.
HANDICAP	Working with a disadvantage of some fashion.
HOLE	Complete.
HOLE IN ONE	Completed in short time.
IRON	Pressing forward.

PAR	Doing what is expected.
SCORE CARD	Keeping track of time and accomplishments.
TEE	Holding something up.

RUGBY

BALL	Getting bounced around.
BACK LINE	Can see alignment, of situation.
BACKS	Going as far back as you can go.
BLIND SIDE FLANKER	You cannot see what is coming regarding female energy.
CENTER	Get right in the middle of things.
CHAMPIONSHIP	You are winning.
CHIP KICK	(D) You have a small piece of what needs to be booted out.
CLEATS	Making a sharp point.
COACH	(D) More than one is hurting or aching, you are in charge.
COMMANDS (Types)	(D) Man moving forward. Warrior energy.
BAGGAGE	Weighed down by old stuff.
CROUCH	See what is below, look down.

PAUSE	Slow down and see the bigger picture, take a breather.
TOUCH	Feel, make physical contact.
DEFENSE	Defend what is rightfully yours.
FLAG	A warning of some kind. Check the Color (Red = Danger or stop, Yellow = take with caution, Green = go and White = infraction or surrender).
KNEE KICK	Only moving with half of your power.
FRONT ROVER	(D) Scouting things out in front.
FULLBACK	You are fully protected.
HOOKER	(D) Grab in the female energy.
GOAL POST	(D) You have announced your desires.
INFRINGEMENT	Someone is in your space.
JERSEY NUMBERS	
Number 8	Visionary, in charge Type person.
Number 9	The closer, completer, finished.
KNOCK OUT	In the dark, no clarity, can not see.
LOCKS	Standing still, not going anywhere, tied up for awhile.
LOOP	Coming around full circle.

MAULS	Everything is being handled in a large way.
OFFENSE	Move forward, speak your truth, strut your stuff.
PASSING	Your part is done or completed, turning it over to someone else.
PENALITY KICK	Being responsible for your own actions.
QUICK TAP	A fast way of getting someone's attention.
QUICK THROWS	Fast energy, (Thought).
RAKING	(See Baseball)
REFEREE	Someone is blowing the whistle on you.
SCORE	Making points.
SCREW POINT	You are getting your point across.
SCRUMHALF	Fighting for your half of something.
SCRUM TIME	There is a time to fight for beliefs.
SIN BIN	Watch out, you are hurting someone here.
TACKLE	Jump on it.
TIMEOUT	Take a breather.
TIMEKEEPER	Someone keeping track of the duration of a situation.

WHEEL	Moving right along.	
WHISTLE	Listen up.	
WINGS	Things are moving upward, things are now able to fly.	
YELLOW CARD	Watch out you are being warned.	

SOCCER

BALL	(See Basketball)
CLEATS	Making a deep impression.
DRIBBLING	(See Basketball)
DRILLS	(See Basketball)
HEAD SHOT	(D)Thinking about shooting with the power of the brain.
HOCKEY SACK	Balancing of little things.
UGGLING	One has a lot on his plate.
PASSING	(See Rugby)
SET UP	Getting ready to make a score.
SHIN GUARD	Major protection, being able move forward.

SWIMMING

BACK STROKE	You are moving forward without really looking. Back up and observe the entire picture.

BELLY FLOP	Someone is making a big splash, yet one might get hurt.
BREAST STROKE	Keep abreast of event around you.
BUTTERFLY STROKE	Lighten up, energy flung all over the place. Measure of time line. What stage are you in?
CAP	Protection against unwanted thoughts.
DIVING BOARD	Bouncing, A need to get higher.
FLIP	A need to make a 180 degree turn.
FLOATERS	Keep your head up.
FLOAT	Rest awhile. Enjoy the view.
GOGGLES	Help seeing with clarity.
LANES	Setting Boundaries.
MEDAL	Your reward for work well done.
OLYMPICS	The highest, attainment goals have been achieved.
POOL	Being in the flow of life.
PUSH OFF	Getting an extra boost or ready to begin.
RINGS	Dive deeper into situation.
SIDE STROKE	Out of balance. You are tilted, one side is weighted more then the other, take a breather.

STARTING BLOCK	A designated place in which to begin.
SWIMMING SUITS	Protection from the unexpected outer elements.
TIMER	Designates time spent on event or with a person.
TEAMS	Cooperation with peers, finding perfect alignment with partner.

TENNIS

ACE	One of something.
BREAK POINT	No ties here.
CENTER LINE	(See Basketball)
CLAY COURT	The basic playing space.
DOUBLES	Two people on the same side. Partners, mirror image.
DROP SHOT	The loss of something or someone.
DEUCE	Two of something.
FOOT FAULTS	Watch where you move next.
GRASS COURT	Soft place to play.
LOB	Just getting higher then dumping it.
MATCHES	Starting up of more than one of something.

NET	Division of properties or space, getting caught.
OVERHEAD SERVE	High degree or level of serving.
RACQUET	Lots of strings attached.
SERVING	Making something happen for the good.
SETS	Gathering of more than one, firm in a space.
SINGLES	Only one can act at a time.
SPIN	Turning things around quickly.
UMPIRES CHAIR	Tall authority looking down on a situation.
VOLLY	Indecision of some sort, the going back and fourth.

CHAPTER 11
MISCELLANEOUS

ALLERGY	Uncomfortable with a person or situation, there is a blockage, warning to look deeper into what is surrounding at this time.
ASPIRIN	Someone or something is giving you a headache, time to quiet yourself and take a break.
BABIES BREATH	Celebration, breath of fresh air.
BAG OF RAGS	There is a big mess to clean up.
BEACH BALL	Lighten up and play more, someone is full of hot air, inflated ego involved.
BOOMERANG	Watch out for your thoughts are returning. What you sow you reap.
BUBBLE WRAP	Feeling very protected.
BURROWING IN	Aggravating noise, cold feeling.
THE REAR CABOOSE	If no caboose on train means never ending continue on, if caboose, completion of some kind.
CAMERA	Documenting event, visual statement, remembering, zooming in to get a closer look.
CARNIVAL (Tilt a Wheel)	You are spinning around, being taken for a ride.

CELTIC CROSS	Sign of guidance, valuable information is being given.
CHAMBER CHOIR	Sing, many good things coming your way.
CHAOS	Lack of focus or direction, confusion.
CHEEP SEATS	Usually the person is not feeling worthy of receiving, you might want to up grade your thoughts and vibrations to a higher level.
CLOCK	Time to take action, to go, stop.
CLOCK WIND UP	Someone is all wound up, release.
COFFIN	Dead issue, can't breath, decision closed and the deal is sealed, spitting up of flem.
CRAYONS	Multitasked, sees the brightness in all things.
CHARIOT RACE	One person working by themselves to complete task quickly.
CALLIOPE	Letting off a little steam, need for your voice to be heard. Someone is full of hot air.
CHARGE CARDS	Movement, you hold the ACE card in the deck of life, time to move forward.
CHEWING CUD	Still trying to digest information.

CHICKEN POX	The spreading of a situation that bothers or is under your skin, you are rather irritated.
CHOP STICKS	Take little steps, catch the small little miracles in life.
CONFERENCE TABLE	A need for discussion, different opinions.
CONDUIT	Add additional flavor to situation, the adding of more energy.
CORN ON THE COB	Take small deliberate steps, stay focused.
CREMATION	Dead issue, heated discussion.
CREAM OF TARTAR	See the sweetness in the bitter lessons of life.
CROP DUSTER	Flying low, healing.
DOWSING ROD	Look a little deeper into the issue.
EMBARRASSED	(D) Caught with your pants down. Not prepared for the words spoken.
ERASER	Identifying mistake, getting rid of situation, clean slate, fresh start.
FALSE TEETH	Someone not giving you the truth. Need for making an impression on someone.
FLIP CHART	Switching directions.
FLUTE	Moving up gently in life, being soft with yourself going up the emotional scale.

FOUNTAIN	You are in the flow, rising higher.
GRANDSTAND	Many are supporting you.
KALEIDOSCOPE	Seeing something change right before your eyes.
LADDER	Way of determining place on the scale of question being asked, look at which direction you are heading.
LIGHT BULBS	Depends on the wattage, being able to see how warm or hot your thoughts might be.
MOLOTOV COCKTAIL	A small explosion is at hand, explosive energy.
MATCHES	The striking up of something hot.
MAX A MILLION	You are getting the maximum deal for your money.
MEGAPHONE	The need to listen Big time.
MISTLETOE	Sweet kisses, shooting rockets.
MONOCLE	Only seeing one point of view.
MOOSE HEAD HANGING	Hang in there, it will change, this to shall pass.
MOTION PICTURES	A visionary, clairvoyant abilities, seeing what is happening in your present life, and how do you see the ending.

MOUNTAIN	Identify where you are on the mountain, the top indicating completion and or you are on top of the situation at hand.
MUSIC	Tone, your vibration, (Listen for the Type of music, example The Blues, sadness, feeling down).
MUSTARD SEED	Person is a wise one and very intelligent.
NICKELODEON	Dance with the music of life.
NOMAD	(D) Do not be angry.
OWNERS MANUAL	May need a tune up, you might need to see your Dr. or Dentist, be in gratitude for what you already own.
PTOMAINE POISONING	Person is releasing junk from their system.
RACE CAR	Move quickly, time is an issue here.
RAINBOW	Represents the human aura. A cleaning has taken place, prosperity.
RINGS OF FIRE	You have just gone through a gateway.
RUDOLPH	Leadership, moving quickly.
SCAB	Protection, a healing, a cover up, need to look at the core issue at hand.
SCISSORS	Cutting a deal.
S&H GREEN STAMPS	Stamp of approval.

SMOKING	Depends on what, Cigars, Cigarettes Menthol Type, it is clouding your vision of some kind.
STEPPING STONE	Strong footing, you are being guided on your path.
SWITCHBLADE KNIFE	Look at both sides of situation.
TATTOO	Documenting impressionable thoughts.
TEA CUP	Can only digest small amounts of hot stuff, somewhat fragile.
TEETH MARK	Someone wanting to make an impression, putting ones mark on a situation.
TELESCOPE	Get a closer look, you can view things not seen before, snooping energy.
TIGHTROPE	Need for balance, to focus looking straight ahead, do not stop now.
TIRES	Allowing movement, check to see if moving forward or in reverse.
TIPS	Good information, rewards for service.
U-TURN	Changing directions now going the other way.
TOILET PAPER ROLL	Not comfortable in the role one is playing in present situation.
TOILET SEAT COVER	Temporary protection.
TOMMY HAWK	Cut the ties that bind you. (D) watch a man named Tom like a hawk.

TOOTHPASTE	Clean up words, speak your truth.
TOUPEE	Covering something up.
TREE HOUSE	Observe what is going on around your home.
TRAMPOLINE	Feeling high look for what comes jumping into your space.
TOADSTOOL	Looking for protection.
TRAIN TRACKS	You are on your lives path moving right along.
TURTLE NECK	Slow down, check to see if there is What might you be hiding from?
T.V. PROGRAM	Types of programs describes action to take. Example Comedies. You need to lighten up and laugh.
VENOM	You are around a toxic person or situation.
VENT	Let your emotions out, a need of a fresh new thought.
WADING POOL	Stepping into shallow waters. Watch your step.
WAND	Look for great miracles coming your way, magical things.
WHEEL OF FORTUNE	Luck and good fortune is here for you now.

WRIST WATCH	Time to wind things up, something is time sensitive.
YELLOW TAXI	Needing a lift of some sort, third chakra, loosing your power.
PHRASES CHALK TALK	A temporary situation that can change at any time, can clearly be erased.
COUCH POTATO	Lack of energy for life.
DUMMY	Comes across as not knowing.
GALLOPING GOURMET	Bringing in joy and happiness into life, Nature supplying nutrition down to cellular memory.
GO WITH THE FLOW	Surrender, give it up and release, don't be fighting the current.
GOING GOING GONE	You are the winner, watch out for your energy depletion.
KNOCK KNOCK	Simple reminder to wake up.
LAST TANGO IN PARIS	It takes two people to make this situation to happen.
LOST AND FOUND	Check your balance on the emotional scale.
MILK TOAST	(D) A pure old softy, or a person who has no backbone, crumbles at the sight of any conflict.
NITWIT	A person with lesser intelligence.
RELAX	Lighten up on self or situation. Just Be.

ROSE CLORED GLASSES	Seeing things from a loving heart.
SCRIBBLING OUTSIDE THE LINES OR BOX	Person is a non-conformist, risk taker, strong willed.
SIDE STEPPING	Waits to take action, not feeling safe, not facing something right in front of you.
SLAVE DRIVER	(D) Someone is having you do all the hard someone forcing their will upon you.
SNAP, CRACKLING, AND POP	Snap to it, movement, listen up you are being guided.
TRICK OR TREAT	Look at the attire the person is wearing to see if this is a positive or negative influence in your life.
WISEACREA	Dry whit, very intelligent.

PART VI
CHANGE

That word "CHANGE" is very hard for many of us to swallow. Some parts of our lives are easier than others. What is so very special about this process is that if you are getting answers that are negative and not what you want to live by, not representing the real happy you, then you get to change the vibration of it and help your self CHANGE and evolve as a spirit. We are very powerful beings, and with a little effort on your part, you can turn aspects of your life completely around and make it very positive.

The "Change" comes when we do something different then what we are doing at this moment in time. Change the patterns. Do a "Pattern Interrupt (P.I.).The definition of "Insanity" is continuing to do the same thing over and over again, expecting the results or the situation to be different. A lot of your thought patterns have been ingrained by your parents, family, schools, society, government etc. So ask if they are what you believe or are you running someone else's energy and their belief system ? Be true to YOU.

PART VII
YOU CAN DO IT, YOU CAN DO IT, YOU CAN, YOU CAN. YOU CAN, YOU CAN!

ALL RIGHT START your engines people reading this book. On your mark, get set, GO. This is all about YOU. You have just been given a fresh new complete way and opportunity to grow and evolve as a spirit. The best thing is that you can have a blast, love laugh and enjoy this whole process. The green flag is waving at you letting you know you are on the right track, and the Red stop sign reminds you to stop, take a few breaths and "JUST ASK" once in a while, to remain in balance in alignment and communicate with your God. It is only you holding yourself back from the endless miracles from happening. Fill up your love tank on a regular basis. Remember you are a limitless being. You can do it, you can you can. Let your light shine and be the beacon for us all to see your magnificence. My three year old grandson would applaud himself after completing a task saying with the biggest smile on his face, "I DID IT" Yep, Grandma Sue just did it and I am grateful to all of you for allowing me to share my gifts with you. I look forward to seeing your light.

"Over There" Productions

To order "JUST ASK" or other products and services,

please contact Sue Chandler at

www.overthereproductions.com

Send in any additional words, thoughts, phrases used, regarding your hobbies, or professions and Sue Chandler will channel these and make available on her web site.

Made in the USA
Las Vegas, NV
15 April 2022

47489415R00080